A Year In The Life

Chloe Cunningham

BookLeaf Publishing

Presentation by *BookLeaf Publishing*

Web: www.bookleafpub.com

E-mail: info@bookleafpub.com

ISBN: 9789357211512

First edition 2023

DEDICATION

Dedicated to my Dad, the strongest person I know.

To my Mum, the bravest person I know.

To my Kilian, the kindest person I know.

Thank you for loving and empowering me.

ACKNOWLEDGEMENT

This book is for the every day person. Specifically for all of you who are going through a hard time right now, remember you are not alone and it will get better. Also remember the power of a smile or a simple compliment can go a long way, be kind to one another.

PREFACE

All of the poems recorded in this book are based on true experiences; my experiences. Life can change in an instant, but so can we. This book is the story of my year. Learn from it, reflect on it, think about how you can change another persons life. - The Author

February 25th

As the sun sets in good time
A cool breeze is on the horizon
As the leaves begin to fall
So too will I

The pain was growing
A sharp stab in my stomach
My appendix was crying
But so was my Mum

"Chloe, your Dad has to go on a ventilator"
Any last words?
Dad, I love you
I love you too mate

The pain was going
Deep sorrow grew in its place
Only one thing is for certain
Summer is over

Grief

All four of us are seated
The anxiety of anticipation fills the room
The doctor says "Your Dad isn't going to make it"
I hear sobs, but my body goes numb

When I get home I go to whom I love most
In his embrace I break
Tears like a waterfall
He's not even dead yet, but I grieve

He's not going to be there when I walk down the aisle
He's not going to be there when I have my first kid
He's not going to be there when I open my own business
He's not going to be there

I should have been a better daughter
I should have spent more time with him
I should have made more of an effort
But I'm out of time

Everyday Life

As I sit at home I think of you
Buried in university work I long for sleep
Whilst you sleep in the hospital bed
Fighting for your life

What were you dreaming of?
Going on a holiday, eating a waffle
Or just sitting with Mum having a coffee
I'm just here hoping my car service isn't too
expensive

I go to work each day
I fold clothes and my eyes well with tears
I fight them because I don't want others to know
I'm in pain
You're in the biggest fight of your life and
there's nothing I can do

The ventilator is your life support
Each puff of air fills you up
I lay awake at night breathless, sweating, heart
beating
I long for air

My life carries on

Whilst yours is clinging on
As I butter my toast each morning
All I think of is you

Dear Mum

You are the bravest person I know
In the hardest time of your life
You never stopped loving us
And you never gave up

You went to the hospital everyday
You sat by Dad's side
I saw how much you love him
I hope I find that kind of love

In those secret moments where you showed your tears
All I wanted was to take your pain away
So I sat by your side and embraced you
Knowing that was the most I could do

I want to thank you
You made us feel loved even when you were feeling down
There is no stronger person than you
Mum, I love you

Thank You

Thank you for all your love
For all the hugs and kisses
For listening
For always being there
Thank you Kilian

Thank you for all your support
For staying with us
For showing us love
For all the home cooked meals
Thank you Nanna, Aunty Lynda, Aunty Deb,
and Uncle Matthew
Thank you for caring about us
For all the meals every night
For all the driving
For always checking in
Thank you Alice

Thank you for making an effort
For all the chats
For showing you care
For going out of your way to be there
Thank you Sarah, Allanah, Jess, Cindy, Tom,
Alyssa, and Jomar

24th June

As the nights grow longer
And the days get colder
Hope is on the horizon
As today you come home

After the worst 4 months of our lives
Here you are
As I see you walking towards the house
I am warmed with joy

As you step inside
Like a fish out of water
No more white walls, constant beeping, hospital food
Just silence, Benny boy, family

You are home!
Life will be different from now on
But that's the price I'd pay any day
As long as you are here

New Zealand

Just as your arrive home
I am set to depart
My first time overseas
New Zealand here I come

Day 1

We arrive at night
Nothing to be seen
My body shaking with excitement
Eager to see the next day

The waves crash on the shore
The sun has awaken
I look outside
Ready to take on the day

It was like nothing I had ever seen
Luscious green hills stretch for miles
Elegant rock formations hug the mountains
Fluffy white sheep dance everywhere

The van was silent
We sat there in awe
New Zealand is so beautiful
We can't wait to explore

Dear Best Friend

Where do I begin
There is nothing I want more in life
Than to share new experiences with you
For us to grow, to challenge ourselves, to love

As I sat in that boat
I watched you fall from the cliff
You just bungee jumped for the first time
I am so proud of you

As we drove down Arthur's Pass
We began to see white stuck to the mountains
As you took your first steps in the snow
That big goofy smile made me fall more in love

As we sat in Fergburger
I watched you take your first bite
I promise I will take you back there one day
To eat it all again

Kilian I am so grateful I got to share these moments with you
There is no one else in the world I would rather be with, travel with, eat burgers with

I want to say thank you
Thank you for being you
Thank you for showing me what love is
Thank you for travelling with me
I love you

Snow

We board the bus at the bottom of the mountain
The whiteness grows as we ascend
The beautiful sun rises on the horizon
A real winter wonderland

Like a little kid on Christmas
So eager to hit the slopes
Surrounded by so many people
Engulfed by a sea of colour

Our feet are consumed by the snow
So fluffy and shiny
As we board the ski lift
It's Kilian's first time

We reach the top of the mountain
Full of awe, fear, and excitement
One last look at each other
Off on the green run we go

September 5th

The trees begin to blossom
The flowers paint the earth
The air grows warmer
It's time for something new

There isn't a cloud in the sky
Surrounded by grassy plains
I step up to the tee
Driver in hand

The adrenaline rushes through me
I swing
Slice it to the right of course
But I'm just happy to be here

We walk together
Golf bags on our shoulders
There is no where else I'd rather be
Than playing golf with you

University Student

Halfway through the semester
Man I'm so close
What a year it has been
I'm ready for it to be done

I've tried my very best
Assignment after assignment
All I want is to do is rest
But the workload is never ending

"Uni is the best time of your life"
So why am I always tired and have no friends
I sit in class waiting
Waiting to enter the real world

I am stuck in Earth's purgatory
I crave experiences
But here I am taking notes
Notes I will forget in 6 months time

Uni is a waste of time.

Dad's Birthday

Happy birthday to you
You're turning 52!
I'm so happy you are here
It could have been a very different year

I watched as you sat behind your cake
Your eyes welled with tears
I knew what you were thinking
I was thinking the same thing

You fought so hard this year
You overcame so much
But here you are
Another lap around the sun

Let the tears fall
You should be so proud
Surrounded by your family
We all love you so much

Our Perfect Afternoon

The sun is shining
The birds are singing
Meet me at the river
I want to be with you

Throwing the frisbee back and forth
Constant laughter in between
This is exactly where I want to be
In this moment with you

We reflect on life together
Our ups and downs
Here I feel safe
Comforted by your love and care

As I lay with you on the picnic rug
Warmed by your embrace
I wish we could stay here forever
Our perfect afternoon

My Enemy

You come and go
Sometimes on purpose
Sometimes for no reason at all
But every time you are not welcome

My hands begin to sweat
My stomach fills with nausea
My heart begins to race
I rock back and forth huddled in a ball

"Is he going to get bored of me?"
"Why does she want to be my friend?"
"What if something happens to him?"
"What if I fail?"

It's always with me
Wherever I go
I've grown to hate it so much
But It's a part of me

I'm my own worst enemy

December 25th

I've been looking forward to this
My favourite time of year
Today is December 1st
Summer is finally here

Putting up our Christmas tree
Red, green, and gold
Our house is filled with Christmas cheer
As jingle bells is told

I love this time of year
It is a celebration of love
We reflect on what has been
And what is to come

This year has been confusing to say the least
The most terrifying and amazing year I've had
From almost losing Dad to going to New Zealand
But soon it will be Christmas and we can be thankful for what we have

2022

Well shit
What a year
This year has taught me so much
Shaped me into who I am today

Almost losing Dad
The worst experience of all
I learnt that life can change in an instant
And to always make an effort with those you love most

Going to New Zealand
The best experience of all
I learnt that our beautiful world needs to be explored
And how deeply in love I am with the one who means most

Whilst this year wasn't what I'd hoped
I gained experiences and moments
I lost friends and gained new ones
But through it all I had a family who stood by me and loved me most

2023

As I wait eagerly for the countdown to midnight
I look forward to a new year
This will be a year of new beginnings
As well as a year of growth

In 2023 I wish for good health
I hope my Dad continues to get better
I hope I prioritise my mental health
I hope my family meet our fitness goals

In 2023 I wish for closer friendships
I hope my friendships continue to grow
I hope I build stronger sibling bonds
I hope Kilian and I continue to thrive

In 2023 I wish for a better me
I hope I learn new things
I hope I continue to work hard
I hope I am kinder to myself

www.ingramcontent.com/pod-product-compliance
Lightning Source LLC
Chambersburg PA
CBHW062110140826
49812CB00058B/1218

* 9 7 8 9 3 5 7 2 1 1 5 1 2 *